IT'S LAUGH O'CLOCK

WOULD YOU RATHER?

Easter Edition

With Fun Illustrations

RIDDLELAND

TABLE OF CONTENTS

Riddleland Bonus

Join our **Facebook Group** at **Riddleland for Kids**
to get daily jokes and riddles.

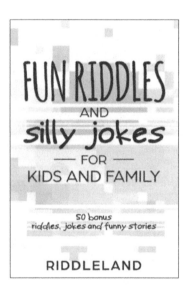

https://pixelfy.me/riddlelandbonus

Thank you for buying this book. As a token of our appreciation,
we would like to offer a special bonus—a collection of 50
original jokes, riddles, and funny stories.

INTRODUCTION

"Egg hunts are proof that your children can find things when they really want."
- Unknown

Are you ready to make some decisions? **It's Laugh O'Clock - Would You Rather? Easter Edition** is a collection of funny scenarios, wacky choices, and hilarious situations which offer alternative endings for kids and adults to choose among.

These questions are an excellent way to get a fun and exciting conversation started. Also, by asking "Why?" after a "Would you Rather . . . " question, learn a lot about the person, including their values and their thinking process.

We wrote this book because we want children to be encouraged to read more, think, and grow. As parents, we know that when children play games, they are being educated while having so much fun that they don't even realize they're learning and developing valuable life skills. "Would you Rather . . . " is one of our favorite games to play as a family. Some of the 'would you rather ...' scenarios have had us in fits of giggles, others have generated reactions such as: "Eeeeeeuuugh, that's gross!" and yet others really make us think, reflect and consider our own decisions.

Besides having fun, playing these questions have other benefits such as:

Enhancing Communication – This game helps children to interact, read aloud, and listen to others. It's a fun way for parents to get their children interacting with them without a formal, awkward conversation. The game can also help to get to know someone better and learn about their likes, dislikes, and values.

Building Confidence – The game encourages children to get used to pronouncing vocabulary, asking questions, and overcoming shyness.

Developing Critical Thinking – It helps children to defend and justify the rationale for their choices and can generate discussions and debates. Parents playing this game with young children can give them prompting questions about their answers to help them reach logical and sensible decisions.

Improving Vocabulary – Children will be introduced to new words in the questions, and the context of them will help them remember the words because the game is fun.

Encouraging Equality and Diversity – Considering other people's answers, even if they differ from your own, is important for respect, equality, diversity, tolerance, acceptance, and inclusivity. Some questions may get children to think outside the box and move beyond stereotypes associated with gender.

Would You Rather?
Easter Edition

How do you play?

At least two players are needed to play this game. Face your opponent and decide who is **Easter Bunny 1** and **Easter Bunny 2**. If you have 3 or 4 players, you can decide which players belong to **Easter Bunny Group 1** and **Easter Bunny Group 2**. The goal of the game is to score points by making the other players laugh. The first player to reach a score of 10 points is the **Round Champion**.

What are the rules?

Easter Bunny 1 starts first. Read the questions aloud and choose an answer. The same player will then explain why they chose the answer in the silliest and wackiest way possible. If the reason makes **Easter Bunny 2** laugh, then **Easter Bunny 1** scores a funny point. Take turns going back and forth and write down the score.

How do you get started?

Flip a coin. The Easter Bunny that guesses it correctly starts first.

Bonus Tip:
Making funny voices, silly dance moves or wacky facial expressions will make your opponent laugh!

Most importantly:

Remember to have fun and enjoy the game!

Would You Rather...

Go to school dressed as a tie-dyed
Easter bunny

walk around school all day with
a rotten egg cracked on top of your head?

Sleep sitting on a nest of fragile duck eggs
that need to be kept warm

OR

spend an afternoon picking up little rabbit
poos from all over your yard?

Would You Rather...

Walk around for a day
with a shoe full of speckled jellybeans

wear shoes made from puffy marshmallow
bunny rabbits?

Be trapped for one day inside
a giant milk chocolate Easter bunny

get a giant milk chocolate Easter bunny in your
Easter basket with both of its ears bitten off?

Would You Rather...

Be a vegetarian and only eat things like carrots and lettuce just like the Easter Bunny

be addicted to sugar and only eat sugar cookies like Santa Claus?

Eat all your food by getting it out of plastic Easter eggs

eat food (not Easter eggs) that is dyed pastel colors?

Would You Rather...

Wake up covered in blue speckles all over
your body like a robin's egg

wake up to find yourself sleeping in a robin's nest up
in a tree and have no idea how you got there?

Peck at the ground and eat wriggly
slimy worms

lay a random egg at least once a week
every week?

Would You Rather...

Have Easter basket grass stuck in between
your toes

have a bunch of chick feathers stuck in your hair
that you just can't get out?

Find your Easter basket in a warm oven
so that all your chocolate yummies have melted

find your Easter basket in the freezer
so that all the candy is rock hard?

Would You Rather...

Wear the big awkward
feet of an Easter Bunny costume

OR

wear a big floppy bunny ear headband
to school for a week?

Go on an Easter egg hunt while blindfolded
and unable to see a thing

OR

go on an Easter egg hunt and have your hands
tied behind your back the whole time?

Would You Rather...

Have the webbed feet of a duckling that don't fit into any shoes but help you to be an awesome swimmer

make the quacking sound of a duck every time you open your mouth?

Walk across a playground covered with broken Easter eggshells

play around in a sandbox filled with jellybeans instead of sand?

Would You Rather...

Have crazy green Easter basket grass growing out of your head instead of hair

wear pants made from woven Easter basket material?

Sleep in an Easter basket covered with grass instead of covered by a blanket in your bed

sleep cozy and warm inside an egg waiting to hatch?

Would You Rather...

Wear a thick fluffy Easter Bunny costume
for a whole day and get super sweaty

be picked up from school one day by your mom
dressed up in an Easter Bunny costume?

Make homemade bunny-shaped cinnamon rolls
with raisins for eyes

try to scramble eggs in the shape of little chicks
for breakfast?

Would You Rather...

Have bunny whiskers that constantly
tickle your face

a pink bunny nose that randomly twitches
throughout the day?

See a flurry of fluffy feathers floating around your
bedroom every time you walk into it

hear phantom chirping chick noises every night
as you lay down to go to sleep?

Would You Rather...

Find random clumps of bunny fur
in your clothes every day

find muddy little bunny paw prints all over
your house every day?

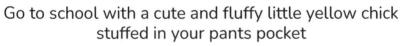

Go to school with a cute and fluffy little yellow chick
stuffed in your pants pocket

try to keep the cute and fluffy little yellow chick stuffed
into your desk so no one sees it all day?

Would You Rather...

Go to school transformed into
a big chocolate Easter bunny

be the only person at your school who
is not a big chocolate Easter bunny?

Have an egg and spoon race where you run with
a raw egg balanced on a spoon

have an egg toss contest where you see who
can catch a raw egg from the farthest distance
without it breaking?

Would You Rather...

Imagine your teacher has turned into a big chocolate bunny every time you look at him or her

be sitting in a desk made entirely out of chocolate?

Spend spring break building and hanging out in the coolest backyard treehouse in your own backyard

going to a week-long camp
of your choice?

Would You Rather...

Take a painting class where you try to paint
the Easter Bunny carrying a basket of Easter eggs

try to make a homemade Easter Bunny using
a bunch of cotton balls, glue, and a carrot?

Skip going trick-or-treating one year
on Halloween and get no candy

get stiffed out of your
Easter basket goodies (no candy)
by the Easter Bunny?

Would You Rather...

Eat only beautifully dyed hard-boiled eggs
for a week after Easter

eat nothing but salty pink Easter ham
for the week after Easter?

Be forced to eat every single piece of Easter candy
in your basket on Easter Sunday

only be able to eat one piece every day
until it is all gone?

Would You Rather...

Have 100 little chocolate Easter bunnies

have one big chocolate Easter bunny that
is as tall as you are?

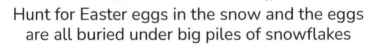

Hunt for Easter eggs in the snow and the eggs
are all buried under big piles of snowflakes

hunt for Easter eggs after a nice spring rain shower
has put all the eggs into little mud puddles?

Would You Rather...

Weave your own Easter basket
out of banana peels

out of dried corn husks from autumn?

Eat a delicious homemade Easter dinner with all your
favorite holiday foods

go to a restaurant's Easter buffet and have a choice of
any kind of food you can imagine, not necessarily your
favorites and not necessarily fresh?

Would You Rather...

Get a piece of Easter basket grass in your mouth
while eating a chocolate egg

get a piece of your own hair in your mouth?

Go Easter egg hunting at night searching
for glow-in-the-dark eggs

go Easter egg hunting after a rainstorm
has washed away most of the eggs' dye?

Would you Rather...

Eat only foods made from chocolate or covered in chocolate for the rest of your life

never be able to eat chocolate again?

Pull the best Easter Prank on your sibling but get in trouble with your parents

spend a long time putting together the best Easter Prank and then it spectacularly backfires?

Would You Rather...

Be required to take a picture of every single
Easter egg you find in a hunt

put them all in a basket and carry them
around with you?

Be followed to school every day by an orderly little
line of fluffy yellow chicks chirping merrily

a hippity hoppity line of little bunnies with
cute floppy ears?

Would You Rather...

Have an Easter lily in your bedroom that looks beautiful but smells bad

have one that smells good but makes you sneeze?

Collect enough honey from beehives to fill up a big jar

snip fresh cut flowers from the garden while being chased by bees who want to collect pollen from your flowers?

Would You Rather...

Grow a cute little cotton ball tail like
a bunny rabbit

lose all but your two front teeth which grow larger and
stick out of your mouth like a little bunny rabbit?

Wake up to see the ground covered with a blanket of
fresh new snow on the first day of spring

be woken up to a rumbly downpouring
thunderstorm?

Would You Rather...

Work at a chocolate factory surrounded by yummy chocolate goodies and smells but not be able to eat chocolate

work at a farm supervising the chicken coops and collecting eggs from the hens every day?

Stuff twenty marshmallow chicks into your mouth

sneeze chocolate milk out of your nose?

Would You Rather...

Find twenty chocolate Easter eggs that
are kind of old and tasteless

one small chocolate Easter egg that tastes
absolutely perfect?

Dye two dozen Easter eggs and only have one of those
eggs look the way that you want

only get to dye one egg and take your chances that it
looks the way that you want?

Would You Rather...

Wear a perfume or cologne that smells like
your favorite flower

one that smells like your favorite candy bar?

Try to guess how many jellybeans are in a jar
and the closest guess wins the whole jar

eat a bunch of funky flavored jellybeans (like tomato
soup) blindfolded and try to guess the flavor?

Would You Rather...

Search through a very large hen house full of smelly chickens to find the one that lays golden eggs

dig into the garbage dumpster every day because someone throws away a fully wrapped king-sized candy bar?

Work at a pet store cleaning out the rabbit cages

scrubbing out the insides of the fish tanks?

Would You Rather...

Decorate your bedroom for Easter by gluing a bunch of minty green Easter basket grass on the walls

by hanging a bunch of real Easter eggs from the ceiling with string and staples?

Play a game of Pin the Cotton Ball (tail) on the Bunny

go bowling using an Easter egg instead of a bowling ball?

Would You Rather...

Sit on a big oval Easter egg instead
of a chair at your desk

play in a sandbox filled with jellybeans at recess?

Get an Easter basket filled with real grass
from your lawn mower bag

one full of plain raw white eggs from the carton
in your refrigerator?

Would You Rather...

Perform the chicken dance in front of the whole school while dressed in a feathered chicken costume

the bunny hop while
dressed in a giant rabbit costume?

Get an Easter basket full of hard and chewy fruit flavored jellybeans

get an Easter basket full of soft and sugary licorice-only jellybeans?

Would You Rather...

Eat a special Easter meal of two thick slices of salty ham with one piece of buttered bread sandwiched in between

eat a sandwich made from two slices of buttered bread with a bunch of jellybeans stuck in between?

Paint Easter eggs with leaves from the trees outside

by using pieces of grass from your yard?

Would You Rather...

Walk to school by hopping
like a bunny

by waddling the whole way like a duck?

Spend one Easter filling in for the Easter Bunny and
spending your whole night before Easter sneaking around
hiding Easter baskets for kids

spend all day on Easter looking for your Easter basket
and not being able to find it?

 **Would You Rather...**

Have a body that is like a big oval pastel-colored plastic Easter egg

hair that is green and crazy like
a big handful of Easter basket grass?

Crack every single one of your Easter eggs
as you're dying them

open up a dozen raw eggs and find half of them are
cracked before you can even dye them?

Would You Rather...

Try to make a polka dot dyed Easter egg by using a white crayon to draw perfect little circles

try to make a striped dyed Easter egg by drawing perfectly straight lines all around your egg?

Play a game of hopscotch with a very bouncy rabbit

double Dutch jump rope with two energetic rabbits?

Would You Rather...

Accidentally dye a carton full of eggs
that have not yet been hard boiled

find a smelly boiled Easter egg in June
that no one found before?

Play dodgeball in gym class using a bunch of real eggs
that explode yolks at you when you get hit

a bunch of plastic eggs that are filled with jellybeans and
pop open showering you with jellybeans?

Would You Rather...

Have a pet bunny rabbit that
poops chocolate chips

chocolate covered raisins?

Go on an Easter egg hunt where all the eggs are camouflaged
to their surroundings (eggs in the grass are green, etc.)

go on an Easter egg hunt where all the eggs are rotten,
smelly, easy to find, and not at all fun?

Would you Rather...

Grow beautiful and fragrant flowers
in your garden

grow delicious and nutritious vegetables
in your garden this spring?

Pay someone to hunt for your Easter basket by giving
them one-fourth of your candy out of the basket

by giving them the money that the tooth fairy leaves
you for your next four lost teeth?

Would You Rather...

Fall on the ground and get mud plus grass stains all over the knees of your pants

fall on the ice and get holes in both knees of your pants?

Spend all night crouched under the couch in your living room trying to catch the Easter Bunny

spend all night huddled in the bottom of your chimney waiting for Santa to slide down?

 **45**

Get licorice-flavored jellybeans

coconut-flavored jellybeans if your Easter basket
could only be filled with one flavor?

Go out for recess on a spring day after it's just rained,
and all of the playground equipment is wet

go out for recess on a cold spring day where everything
is coated with a layer of ice?

Would You Rather...

Listen to a story about how your Grandma or Grandpa
spent Easter when they were a kid

how your mom or dad spent Easter
when they were a kid?

Carry a backpack full of unboiled Easter eggs

a backpack full of foil-wrapped chocolate Easter eggs
to school on a warm day?

Would You Rather...

Drive around in a car that looks like
a giant Easter egg

in a car that looks like a giant Easter basket?

Be in Haux, France, on Easter Monday and
eat part of an omelet that uses over 4,500 eggs
and feeds over 1,000 people

eat an omelet for breakfast at home
every single day for a year?

Would You Rather...

Break up a squawking fight between a pair of birds
in a tree outside your bedroom window

break up a chicken fight that breaks out
in a hen house?

March down your street dressed in your fanciest clothes
for your neighborhood's Easter Parade
on Easter morning

get caught outside searching for Easter eggs
in your pajamas?

Would You Rather...

Get a very long piece of green Easter basket grass wrapped around your pinkie toe inside of your sock

a very clingy piece of green Easter basket grass that you just can't shake off your fingers?

Spill a mug full of Easter egg dye on your favorite shirt

spill a mug of Easter egg dye all over your hands leaving them stained for days?

Would You Rather...

Color Easter eggs using
a bunch of broken crayon pieces

a bunch of dried out markers?

Wake up one morning to find a bunch of Easter basket grass
in your belly button with a robin nesting in the middle of it

wake up one morning in the tree outside your window
sitting on a nest of robin's eggs?

Would You Rather...

Put on an Easter Bunny suit after someone
got really hot and sweaty in it

get the head part of the Easter Bunny costume stuck on
your face for an hour after you should be done wearing it?

Roll head over heels like a tucked-in hedgehog
down a grassy green hill

dog paddle your way across a duck pond?

Would You Rather...

Pluck the petals off a bundle of eight daisies,
one by one

count every piece of Easter basket grass
in your basket?

Go to the White House and participate in the official
Easter egg roll with other kids

go to a park and take part in an Easter egg hunt
with other kids?

Would You Rather...

Ride your bike to school when there
is still snow on the ground

try to ride your skateboard to school
on an icy day?

Dye all your Easter eggs the same color,
whichever color you choose

have to dye all of your Easter eggs the same color,
but one that someone else
chooses for you?

Would You Rather...

Get an Easter basket full of 500 pennies

one plastic Easter egg with a $5 bill in it?

Go to Corfu, Greece, the day before Easter when lots of people stand on their balconies and literally throw pots out onto the street

stand by yourself on your porch or deck and throw pots out onto your yard?

Would You Rather...

Eat a cheese Easter egg instead
of a chocolate one

eat a purely dark chocolate Easter egg?

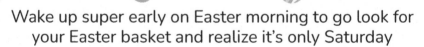

Wake up super early on Easter morning to go look for
your Easter basket and realize it's only Saturday

oversleep on Easter morning and find your little brother or
sister has found your basket and eaten a bunch of the candy?

Would You Rather...

Listen to the sound of the rain falling on your roof but feel like it's falling on your head

the sound of a strong wind blowing against your wall but feel like it's blowing your hair?

Plant a garden filled entirely with your favorite flower

a garden with tons of different colored and scented flowers?

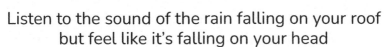

Would You Rather...

Feel the warm sun on your face after
a long cold winter while wearing a tank top

feel the gentle breeze against your skin while
wearing a pair of shorty shorts?

Eat a donut covered from top to bottom
with coconut flakes

eat a glazed doughnut that has raisins all over
the inside of it?

Craft a birdhouse out of a smelly
old milk carton

out of a sticky old soda bottle?

EWW...SO STICKY...

Make a Ukrainian Easter egg by poking holes in both ends of
a raw egg with a needle and blowing out the yolk and then
spending hours decorating an intricate design on the egg

spend hours picking up, by hand, every single piece of
Easter basket grass that you accidently dumped on your
living room floor?

Would you Rather...

Draw a self-portrait in chalk outside
on a sidewalk

fingerpaint a self-portrait on paper using
melted Easter egg chocolate?

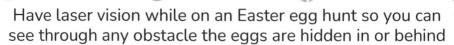

Have laser vision while on an Easter egg hunt so you can
see through any obstacle the eggs are hidden in or behind

have really long stretchy arms that can reach out and
snatch eggs that you see far away?

Would You Rather...

Get stuck going birdwatching with your grandparents
and end up getting bird poop on your sleeve

get your finger bit by a duck while
trying to feed it some breadcrumbs?

Go on an Easter Egg hunt
in a field full of brightly colored flowers

in a huge mansion with fifty different rooms?

Would You Rather...

Read your favorite springtime book inside a cool hollowed-out log near your house

read your favorite Easter book after climbing up into a cozy tree?

Mow the growing tall green grass in your yard

shovel a few inches of snow from your driveway and sidewalks on the first day of spring?

Would You Rather...

Be the last one to jump in the pool

the first person to find a golden egg
in an Easter egg hunt?

Wake up before the sun on Easter morning to search
for your Easter basket but not be able to see anything
because of all the eye boogers in your eyes

be so tired that you sleep the entire day of Easter
away and receive no candy?

Would You Rather...

Try to build a rock sculpture with a bunch of round egg-shaped rocks that keep toppling over

try to see through a pair of sunglasses with dirty fingerprints all over them?

Build a treehouse that is protected from invasion by birds and critters

one that is protected from invasion by your siblings and parents?

Would You Rather...

Have one of the straps of your backpack totally rip off on your way to school scattering Easter candy on the floor

have one of your shoelaces bust in half while you're on your way home from school meaning it takes you longer and a sibling will eat some of your Easter candy?

File your fingernails down
on the bark of a tree

brush your teeth by gnawing
on a tree twig?

Would You Rather...

Dye your Easter eggs using natural foods
like spinach juice and boiled beets

by crushing flower petals and smearing them
all over the boiled eggs?

Spend Easter with your family doing
fun family activities

spend Easter with friends having Easter Egg
hunts and eating candy together?

Would You Rather...

Braid friendship
bracelets out of Easter basket grass

twist a bunch of foil chocolate egg wrappers into
friendship necklaces?

Sleep curled up in the center of a very large flower
that tucks you into its petals at night

sleep next to a wooly lamb who shares her woolen
warmth with you like a blanket?

Would You Rather...

Hear the sound of a bee buzzing
by your ear all day long

the sound of a seashell in your ear while
you're trying to fall asleep?

Dye your Easter eggs by holding them in your mouth
and dunking your face into a cup of dye

dye your Easter eggs by holding them with your fingers
and dunking them into a cup of dye?

Would You Rather...

Find money from another country
in your Easter basket

find candies you don't recognize from
other countries in your Easter basket?

Be responsible for the Easter Bunny tripping over a mess
in your house and twisting his ankle

be responsible for Santa Claus breaking off a tooth
on a too-hard sugar cookie?

Would You Rather...

Find a chocolate Easter bunny with your face on it,
in your Easter basket

a bunch of marshmallow chicks with your brother
or sister's face on them?

Spend spring break doing a deep spring clean
of your bedroom

spend spring break doing a deep dive into
spring yard chores with your parents?

Would You Rather...

Only taste peppermint toothpaste flavor
any time you eat anything chocolate

use toothpaste that tastes like your least favorite
flavor of jellybeans?

Build a fort out of pillows and blankets in the springtime
with nothing to hook them together

try to build a hideout using branches that
have no leaves because it's winter?

Would You Rather...

Catch sight of the Easter bunny running away from your house and see that he wasn't wearing any clothes

watch a chicken laying an egg?

Paint ugly rocks with sayings of kindness to hide for others to find

paint cracked eggs to hide on the playground for your friends to find?

Would You Rather...

Find a bunch of muddy footprints all over
your bedroom floor

find blobs of green jello all over your
bedroom floor?

Be dragged around to a bunch of spring garage sales
early on a Saturday morning

wake up early on a Saturday morning to drag trash bags
out of the house after spring cleaning?

Would You Rather...

Work on a computer with a keyboard
made from chocolate

use a computer mouse made from chocolate?

Wake up on Easter morning only to find that your siblings
put all their coconut jellybeans into your basket

that someone has bit one ear off every chocolate
Easter bunny in your basket?

Would You Rather...

Have a family of chicks nesting underneath your bed

a family of rabbits nesting in the clothes in your closet?

Paint a masterpiece using brushes and different thicknesses of mud from your yard

create a mosaic (pieced together art) by gluing pieces of colored eggshells onto a sheet of paper?

Would You Rather...

Touch your hair with sticky marshmallow covered hands

 OR

melted chocolate covered hands?

Spend two hours going to the grocery store for carrots and then leaving a carrot trail around your house for the Easter Bunny

OR

three hours making homemade sugar cookies for Santa Claus's cookie plate?

Would You Rather...

Wear a pair of shoes made from
plastic Easter eggs

wear socks made from cotton balls?

Go on an Easter egg hunt at your school playground with
all the rest of the kids at your school at the same time

go on an Easter egg hunt where
you compete alongside kids and adults
to find the most eggs?

Would You Rather...

Find your Easter basket stuck
in a big gooey mud puddle

frozen into a yellow snowbank?

Get a different colored Easter basket every year
with different candies in it

get the same exact colored Easter basket with
the same exact amount and kind of candies in it?

Would You Rather...

Be covered in the pretty,
soft yellow fluff of a little chick

have the long floppy ears of a bunny rabbit?

Make windchimes out of used forks and spoons
from your school's cafeteria

make a windchime out of eggshells painted
with metallic paint?

Would You Rather...

Be able to hop, leap, and bound everywhere you go like a bunny

have a cute little fluffy white tail coming out of your behind like a bunny?

Compete in a swinging contest with your teacher at recess, the winner gets an Easter egg

at a park after school with your mom or dad?

Would You Rather...

Everything you eat for the month of April taste like coconut

everything you smell for the month of April smell like a beachy fresh bottle of coconut sunscreen?

End every sentence by saying "That's egg-citing!"

begin every sentence with "I'm hoppy to report"?

Would You Rather...

Be able to jump over cars and playground equipment like a giant Easter bunny

be able to squeeze through tiny spaces like cracks in a fence like a tiny Easter chick?

Throw an Easter party with a bunch of hip-hoppy bunny rabbits

with a bunch of chirpy techno baby chickens?

Would You Rather...

Have a basket of beautifully decorated
Easter eggs that smell rotten

a bunch of really ugly duckling decorated
Easter eggs that are filled with chocolate?

Spend an afternoon picking fragrant daisies
at a flower garden

mowing yards for people in your neighborhood?

Would You Rather...

Spend an afternoon hanging colored plastic Easter eggs on trees in your front yard

OR

spend your afternoon hiding a bunch of dyed hard-boiled eggs all around your yard?

Put on a puppet show by coloring your fingers with Easter egg dye

OR

creating finger puppets out of painted eggshells?

84

Would You Rather...

Get an Easter basket filled with wet spaghetti instead of grass

an Easter basket filled with year-old rock-hard marshmallow bunnies?

Bite into a marshmallow chick that was left over from last Easter

eat a chocolate bunny that someone else took a big bite out of?

Would You Rather...

Have a pet chicken
who lays chocolate eggs for you

a chicken who lays real eggs for you every day?

Spend the day after Easter at the dentist's office because
of all the sugar you ate on Easter

spend the day after the 4th of July at the ear doctor
because you were sitting too close to the fireworks show?

Would You Rather...

Drink a big glass of water that is clear
but tastes like chocolate

 OR

eat a big chocolate bunny that looks and smells
delicious but like water has no taste?

Eat a piece of toast covered with
shaved coconut

 OR

get an edible Easter basket made
from chocolate?

Would You Rather...

Wear a big fancy flower-covered Easter hat
that attracts bees to your head

one covered in chocolate eggs which melt
in the sun and drip into your eyes?

Dress up as a neon green Easter bunny and not get
recognized as the Easter bunny

dress up as a fuzzy little hot pink chick?

Would You Rather...

Swim in a giant pool filled with fruity
flavored little jellybeans

in a hot tub filled with melted chocolate bunnies?

Have a jumbo cotton ball stapled to your rear end
like a rabbit's tail

stick a chewed-on piece of pink bubble gum
to the tip of your nose like a bunny nose?

Would You Rather...

Wear a headband with floppy
Easter bunny ears

wear a big fluffy Easter Bunny cotton tail
to school for a whole day?

Go to see your favorite baseball team play a game
on opening day of baseball season

go to the swimming pool on the opening day
of summer swimming?

Would You Rather...

Run around the park trying
to catch butterflies with a net

trying to catch tadpoles with your bare hands
on a beautiful spring day?

Spend an afternoon feeding smelly ducks
at the pond

spend an afternoon digging acorns for
the twitchy squirrels at the park?

Would You Rather...

Be able to shoot plastic eggs
out of your mouth

jellybeans out of your belly button
on command?

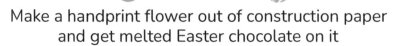

Make a handprint flower out of construction paper
and get melted Easter chocolate on it

let out a big juicy sneeze all over
your paper flower?

Would You Rather...

Celebrate the first day of spring by flying
a kite on a day with barely a breeze

by jumping in puddles and getting mud all up
the back of your clothes and in your shoes?

Spill your bottle of bubbles
before you can even blow one bubble

get a hole in your kite
before you can send it up in the air?

Would You Rather...

Have speckled blue eyes
like a robin's egg

fluffy blond hair like a small chick?

Spill a glass of orange juice on your
Easter Sunday best clothing

get a marshmallow rabbit squished under
the seat of your pants or dress?

Would You Rather...

Try to climb to the top of a tree that doesn't have its leaves yet

try to climb to the top of a tree that is thickly covered with leaves?

Find your Easter basket on Easter morning and find eggs made from chalk in it

eggs made from clay in the basket?

Would You Rather...

Have a pet lamb who follows you to school
every day and sits beside your desk

have a pet rock who you drag along
by a leash wherever you go?

Glue together
a life-sized lamb out of cotton balls

make a blanket to snuggle under by gluing together
tissues from an entire box of Kleenex?

Would You Rather...

Paint all your Easter eggs with cups of paint and a paintbrush instead of dipping them into cups of dye

shoot paintballs at your Easter eggs from across the yard?

Start summer break the day after Easter

end summer break the day after the 4th of July?

Would You Rather...

Stick two boiled Easter eggs in your mouth
at the same time

stuff a whole package of marshmallow rabbits
in your mouth at the same time?

Try to skip a bunch of thick,
round stones across a pond

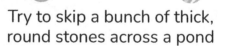

try to build a sandcastle with
sand that's bone dry?

Would You Rather...

Take a walk outside on a cloudy and rainy day
without an umbrella or raincoat

spend an afternoon out in the bright sunshine
without any sunscreen?

Wash your hair with fruity jellybean
scented shampoo

brush your teeth with licorice
flavored toothpaste?

Would You Rather...

Get rained on during
the middle of your spring picnic

drop your sandwich into a mud puddle
during the picnic?

Go to school on Easter if you could have
a longer spring break

have your school's spring break
be part of your Easter holiday break?

Would You Rather...

Have a caterpillar crawl up
the sleeve of your shirt

a butterfly become tangled in your hair?

Grow whiskers overnight that grow back
every time you shave them off

walk around school every day making bunny ears
on everyone you're near?

Would You Rather...

Eat chocolate candy that makes your lips, teeth, and tongue turn black

eat jellybeans that turn your lips, teeth, and tongue green?

Pay a quarter for each piece of chocolate you eat on Easter morning

get paid a quarter for each piece of chocolate you eat on Easter morning?

Would You Rather...

Celebrate Easter in the middle of summer where your chocolate eggs turn into little brown puddles

celebrate Easter in the middle of winter where your chocolate eggs are frozen like little brown ice cubes?

Get tangled up in your kite's string
and fall on the ground

get hit in the leg by a jump rope end that
came loose from your hand?

Would You Rather...

Have brown melted chocolate stuck underneath your fingernails

have a bunch of brown dirt stuck underneath your fingernails?

See who can roll an Easter egg the farthest down a sidewalk

see who can bounce a marshmallow chick the highest off the floor?

Would You Rather...

Dip your bare toes in a green slimy looking pond

dig your bare hands deep into a squishy brown mud puddle?

Go on a field trip to the museum and get lost in the dinosaur display

a field trip to the library and get lost in a favorite Easter book?

Would You Rather...

Get sticky marshmallow creme
on the screen of your phone

stuck in the keys of your computer keyboard?

Collect your family's
used toilet paper tubes

discarded dirty eggshells to plant vegetable
seedlings in for your class garden?

Would You Rather...

Play a game of soccer by kicking around an extra-large Easter egg

OR

play a game of golf by hitting Easter eggs around the course?

Celebrate Easter with the Easter Toad instead of the Easter Bunny

OR

be visited by Belsnickel on Christmas Eve instead of Santa Claus?

Would You Rather...

Roll around in a field of daisies and come out smelling like a rose

roll around in a field of tulips and come out smelling like a daisy?

Go to school on Easter but get a bunch of candy all day long

get Easter off from school but not get any candy all day long?

Did You Enjoy The Book ?

If you did, we are ecstatic. If not, please write your complaint to us and we will ensure we fix it.

If you're feeling generous, there is something important that you can help me with – tell other people that you enjoyed the book.

Ask a grown-up to write about it on Amazon. When they do, more people will find out about the book. It also lets Amazon know that we are making kids around the world laugh. Even a few words and ratings would go a long way.

If you have any ideas or jokes that you think are super funny, please let us know. We would love to hear from you.

Our email address is -
riddleland@riddlelandforkids.com

Riddleland Bonus

Join our **Facebook Group** at **Riddleland for Kids**
to get daily jokes and riddles.

https://pixelfy.me/riddlelandbonus

Thank you for buying this book. As a token of our appreciation,
we would like to offer a special bonus—a collection of 50
original jokes, riddles, and funny stories.

CONTEST

Would you like your jokes and riddles to be featured in our next book?

We are having a contest to discover the cleverest and funniest boys and girls in the world!

1) Creative and Challenging Riddles
2) Tickle Your Funny Bone Contest

Parents, please email us your child's "original" riddle or joke. He or she could win a Riddleland book and be featured in our next book.

Here are the rules:

1) We're looking for super challenging riddles and extra funny jokes.

2) Jokes and riddles MUST be 100% original—NOT something discovered on the Internet.

3) You can submit both a joke and a riddle because they are two separate contests.

4) Don't get help from your parents—UNLESS they're as funny as you are.

5) Winners will be announced via email or our Facebook group – **Riddleland for kids**

6) In your entry, please confirm which book you purchased.

Email us at **Riddleland@riddlelandforkids.com**

Other Fun Books by Riddleland
Riddles Series

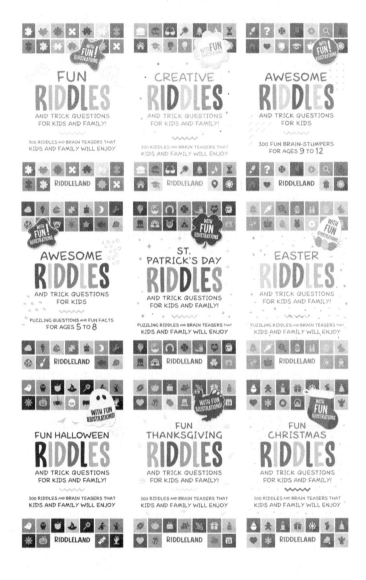

It's Laugh O'Clock Joke Books

Would You Rather...Series

Get them on Amazon or our website at
www.riddlelandforkids.com

114

ABOUT RIDDLELAND

Riddleland is a mum + dad run publishing company. We are passionate about creating fun and innovative books to help children develop their reading skills and fall in love with reading. If you have suggestions for us or want to work with us, shoot us an email at

riddleland@riddlelandforkids.com

Our favourite family quote

"Creativity is an area in which younger people have a tremendous advantage since they have an endearing habit of always questioning past wisdom and authority."

— Bill Hewlett

Made in the USA
Las Vegas, NV
02 April 2022

46757232R00063